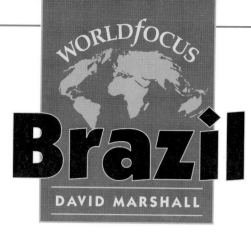

WORLDFOCUS

Brazil

DAVID MARSHALL

Contents

Note to the Reader
Some words in this book are printed in
bold type. This shows that the word is
listed in the glossary on page 30. The
glossary gives a brief explanation of words
that might be new to you.

Introduction

Tropic of Cancer

Equator

Tropic of Capricorn

Brazil is the largest country in the continent of South America. It is also the fourth largest country in the world, with an area of 3,286,500 square miles. It is 10 percent larger than the United States.

Because of its size, Brazil is a land of huge contrasts. There is still uncharted jungle in the Amazon **rain forest**, where over a million different animals and plants live. Some of the plants have great medical value. There are also vast farms in Brazil, with orange groves that stretch as far as the eye can see and crowded cities along the coastline.

The Amazon River rises high in the Andes Mountains and flows east to the Atlantic Ocean. On the way, more than a thousand tributaries flow into the river, swelling its size until at times it looks like an inland sea.

△ **Where is Brazil?**

▽ **Large areas of northeast Brazil suffer from drought, when little or no rain falls in a year. Cactus is used to feed the animals.**

The main features of Brazil's landscape.

Half of Brazil is drained by the Amazon River. For most of its length of 4,004 miles, it flows through tropical rain forest.

The Guiana Highlands, north of the Amazon Basin, have Brazil's highest peaks. Pico de Neblina, or "Cloudy Peak," is 1,871 feet high. The Brazilian Highlands lie to the east and south. This vast plateau is divided by fertile valleys and mountain ranges.

Across all of Brazil, the climate is varied. In the south, the winters are quite cool, and sometimes it even snows. In the northeast, it is always very hot, and the land often looks like a desert. But the tropical rain forest area of the Amazon Basin has one of the steadiest climates in the world. Temperatures there are always about 80–85°F, and it rains all year round. This type of climate is called **equatorial** because it occurs in areas on the Equator, which passes through the Amazon Basin in the north part of Brazil.

The People

Over 150 million people live in Brazil. Throughout Brazil's history, people have come from all over the world to settle there. The population is a mixture of peoples. As well as native **Amerindians**, who have always lived in Brazil, there are European descendants, black Africans brought to Brazil as slaves, and some Japanese. Brazil has the second largest black African population of any country. Many of the different races and peoples have intermarried, which means that Brazilians are one of the most varied peoples in the world.

The first **colonists** from Europe were the Portuguese, who arrived in 1500. At that time there were about 5 million Amerindians in Brazil. Now there are fewer than 200,000.

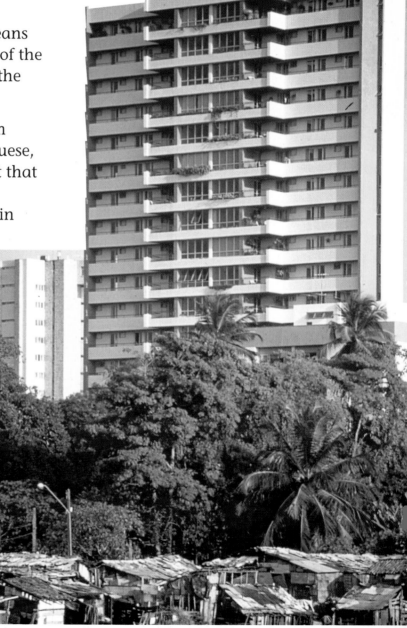

Salvador is a typical Brazilian city. This photograph shows a favela in the foreground and skyscrapers behind.

4

Thousands of Amerindians were killed by the settlers. They were made to work as slaves, and many died because they were cruelly treated. Others died after catching European diseases. Their bodies had no natural resistance to these diseases. The Amerindians of the forest still live by hunting and gathering food and also by farming. They have kept their old traditional way of life, but sometimes they use modern farming techniques.

Every year thousands of new settlers still come to Brazil. The fastest growing city is São Paulo. It has the world's largest Japanese community outside Japan.

In Brazil there is a huge difference between the lives of rich and poor people. Over 20 percent of the Brazilian people cannot read and write. In the United States it is less than 1 percent. Today over 70 percent of Brazilians live in the cities. All the major cities have huge shanty towns, known as **favelas** (slums), where poor people put up houses on vacant land.

The main religion of Brazil is Roman Catholicism. This was brought to Brazil by the Portuguese. There are still Amerindian religions in parts of Brazil. Some Amerindians believe in spirits of people, trees, animals, or non-living things such as waterfalls. Some of the black African people brought their own beliefs to Brazil, which are part of their religion today.

△ **Many black Africans in Brazil are descended from slaves who were brought to Brazil over 300 years ago.**

Where Do People Live?

Over 90 percent of Brazilians live in one-third of the country—mainly in the south and along the coast. The major cities are São Paulo and Rio de Janeiro. São Paulo has a population of over 14,000,000 and is the second largest city in the world. Rio de Janeiro is featured in many travel films because of its beautiful location. It lies just where the hills of the tropical forests roll down to the long sandy beaches of the Atlantic coast.

◄ The cathedral in Brasília is just one of the exciting buildings in Brazil's new capital.

The government of Brazil wanted to encourage people to live in the vast interior of the country. In 1956 it decided to develop a brand new capital city there, called Brasília. The government hoped that moving the capital from Rio de Janeiro, on the coast, to the center of Brazil would help to develop the rest of Brazil. Brasília was built in only three years, and it opened April 21, 1960. It now has a population of over 1,500,000.

Most of the people who live in the country live on plots of land too small to produce enough to feed their families. A few large landowners own enormous expanses of land. Many people are employed on these large farms, but they are usually paid very little. Since the 1950s, thousands of people have moved from villages into the cities of Brazil looking for work. They believe that life in towns will be better.

Brazil's cities are very overcrowded, and there are shortages of houses and jobs. In an attempt to solve these problems, the government has moved some families away from the cities. People have been moved into the Amazon Basin in **colonization** projects. They have been given small farms on land that was once rain forest. Trees have been cut down and the land has been cleared for raising crops. However, the soil is poor, and there are few **nutrients** to feed the growing crops. After two or three years, the soil is exhausted and may be washed away by heavy rainfall. Many of the people have moved back again to the cities after a few years.

There is a lot of land available for farming in Brazil. The government could help families who want to farm by giving out some land and lending people money to buy seeds and tools. However, it prefers to lend money to large landowners. Big landowners depend on large numbers of low-paid workers. They are afraid that if the poor have their own land, it will be hard to find cheap labor. As a result the rich farmers get richer and the poor farmers become poorer.

△ **People who move to the cities have to take any job they can find.**

Agriculture

You can grow almost any crop in Brazil because the climate is so varied. Although many people think of coffee when they think of Brazil, other crops, like soy beans and sugar cane, are just as important. Cacão, tobacco, corn, rice, cotton, and some rubber are also grown. Brazil is the biggest **exporter** of oranges in the world. Sugar cane is used to make an alcohol mixture that is used as fuel for cars!

In the 19th century, rubber was the most important crop in Brazil. It was collected from trees in the forests. In 1876, some seedlings were smuggled out of Brazil to London. They were used to start growing the trees in other countries, mainly in the **Far East**, where the rubber was grown on **plantations**. Brazil's rubber industry could not compete with the new plantations.

Brazil has a huge farming industry. It grows food and raises animals to feed the people of Brazil and to export. Crops are also grown as **raw materials** for Brazil's industries. About one-third of Brazil's exports come from farming.

Many of the people who live in the country do not benefit from this huge farming business. They are the laborers who work on the farms and plantations. Over 12 million people who live in Brazil's countryside are landless, or have so little land that they cannot grow enough food to survive. Over half of all the land in Brazil is owned by only one-tenth of the population. It is this small number of Brazilians who mainly benefit from Brazil's rich agriculture.

▽ **This area was once covered by trees. A farmer is now trying to make a living from the land.**

These Zebu cattle have been brought from India. They can thrive in Brazil's climate.

There is plenty of food in Brazil, but people still go hungry. In the towns and cities, they may not earn enough money to be able to buy food. In the country, poor farmers may not be able to grow enough food to feed themselves and their families. Some of Brazil's produce is also exported. This earns money that is used to repay Brazil's enormous debts to foreign countries.

Over half of Brazil is covered by forest. The Amazon rain forest has the world's greatest number of tropical **hardwoods**. These trees are very valuable. The search for **mahogany** by illegal logging gangs is threatening vast areas of the Amazon forest. The Brazilian government has encouraged landless families and people from the cities to move to land cleared from the forests. This land is often not suitable for growing crops. Also, these people are sometimes driven off their land by wealthy ranchers, who then raise cattle on the land.

Industry

The Itaipú dam contains enough concrete to build a 350-story high-rise building every day for five years.

Since the 1950s, the Brazilian government has led a massive industrial development program. Brazil's main export used to be coffee, but now industry produces two-thirds of all exports. Brazil's main exports are cars, machinery, ships, aircraft, shoes, and iron ore.

Belo Horizonte, São Paulo, and Rio de Janeiro form a triangle, where most of Brazil's manufacturing takes place (see map on page 11).

Brazil has enormous natural wealth. Iron ore, phosphates, uranium, copper, manganese, bauxite, and coal are all waiting to be mined. The government does not have the money to pay for these projects. Brazil is also now into its second gold boom. Gold is being found both underground and in rivers in the Amazon region.

Nearly all the energy in Brazil is produced by **hydroelectric** power stations. To harness energy, a huge dam is built across a river. The dams at Tucuruî in the Amazon Basin and Itaipú on the Paranà River are two of the largest in the world. The giant Itaipú dam cost $20 billion to build. The walls of the dam are the height of a 60-story building. When a dam is built, a large area of land is flooded. At the Itaipú dam, many people were forced off their land as the water rose.

There are many new mines and refineries in Brazil. The picture shows the iron ore mine at Carajàs, which is one of the biggest.

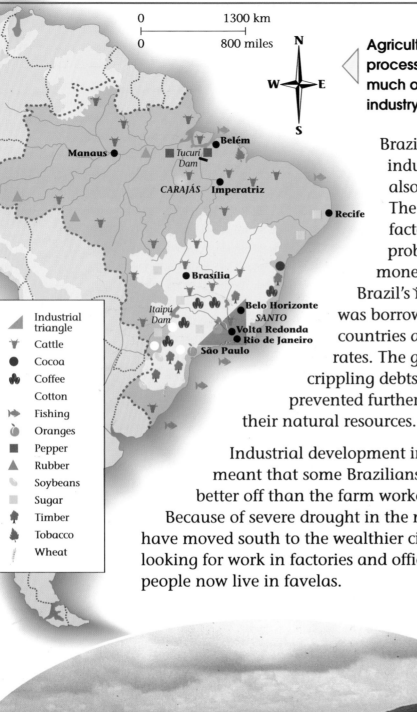

Scale:
0 — 1300 km
0 — 800 miles

N W E S

Legend:
- ◢ Industrial triangle
- Cattle
- ● Cocoa
- Coffee
- Cotton
- ➤ Fishing
- Oranges
- ■ Pepper
- ▲ Rubber
- Soybeans
- Sugar
- Timber
- Tobacco
- Wheat

**Map labels:**
Manaus
Belém
Tucuri Dam
CARAJÁS   Imperatriz
Recife
Brasília
Itaipú Dam
Belo Horizonte
SANTO
Volta Redonda
Rio de Janeiro
São Paulo

Agriculture and food processing are spread across much of Brazil. Most of the industry is in the south.

Brazil's rapid industrialization has also had side effects. The pollution from factories has been a big problem. Also, the money to build many of Brazil's industrial projects was borrowed from other countries at high interest rates. The government now has crippling debts that have prevented further development of their natural resources.

Industrial development in the south has meant that some Brazilians have become better off than the farm workers in the north. Because of severe drought in the north, many people have moved south to the wealthier cities and towns, looking for work in factories and offices. Many of these people now live in favelas.

The Rich and the Poor

In Brazil there are two worlds: a rich world and a poor world.

In the rich world, people are very well off. They work in industry and business, or as doctors, lawyers, or accountants, or are big landowners or merchants. They are better off than most people in the developed world.

In the poor world, people are very poor. They do not have enough to eat, or enough money to buy clothes, shoes, or pay for medicine and school. They get ill more easily and they die younger. The poorest people live in the country and in the favelas of the towns and cities.

The government has tried to use Brazil's natural riches to make money to pay off its huge debts and to make life better for all Brazilians. It has encouraged industry and developed agriculture. This has been quite successful, but the people who have benefited have mainly been those who were already wealthy. Poor people are not much better off, even though Brazil as a whole has become richer.

Most favelas have no garbage collections. Here in Recife, a pig feeds among the trash at the side of the main road.

There have been some huge industrial developments in the country. One is at Carajás in northern Brazil, in Amazonia. The area has an iron ore mine, logging from the rain forest, an aluminum **smelter**, and a good railroad system. The Carajás development involved cutting down an area of forest as big as France in less than ten years. Hundreds of thousands of the poorest Brazilians came to Carajás from all over the country in search of work and land. A nearby village called Imperatríz became a town of nearly half a million people. There were no plans to cope with this sudden growth, and the city grew with no health or sanitation system. While it was being built, Carajás offered some jobs. But there were not enough long-term jobs for all the people who flocked to Imperatríz.

Deforestation means that many Amerindians lose their homes.

The destruction of the rain forest, known as **deforestation**, is seen as a disaster by most people in the rest of the world. For the Amerindians who have lived in the forest for generations, it can mean the end of their traditional way of life. The government has a policy known as **demarcation**, which tries to protect Indian reservations from development. However, many Indian groups have not been able to register their lands, and developers seem to be able to ignore the government's rules.

Brazil needs to find a way to preserve its environment and at the same time make the best use of its natural resources for the benefit of all its people.

Recife

Recife is Brazil's fourth largest city, with a population of over 1,200,000. It is the capital of the state of Pernambuco in the northeast of Brazil. Recife is a port and is sometimes called the Venice of Brazil, because it is a city of water and bridges. Nearby is Recife's sister town of Olinda, which was Brazil's capital before Rio de Janeiro and Brasília.

Recife is big and modern, but more difficult to travel around than many other large cities. The center is a mixture of high-rise offices, old colonial churches, and crowded markets. It is easy for strangers to get lost in the maze of winding, one-way streets. Some of Brazil's most famous artists live in Recife, and it is well known for its painting, sculpture, dance, music, and festivals.

A child sits by the road in a favela, in the Entre Apulso area of Recife.

Recife.

Recife has an airport where many flights from Europe land. Flights bringing Europeans have led to a great many developments for tourists and rich landowners. New nightclubs, restaurants, and hotels have grown up around the beaches of Boa Viagem. The beaches are Recife's biggest tourist attraction.

In the last few years, severe drought in the northeast has caused many crops to fail. Nearly half the sugar cane harvest has been lost. Many people have had to travel long distances, searching for water. The drought has led to over a million people, especially men, moving from the country into the cities, looking for work. Even cities like Recife are suffering from constant water shortages and rationing. New favelas for the migrants have grown quickly and appear almost everywhere. Favela houses are shacks, usually made from wood, corrugated metal sheets, plastic, and cardboard. Very few favelas have running water, electricity, or sewage systems.

△ Favelas have been built on vacant land in Recife. You can see the tall buildings of the city center in the distance.

City Life

In Recife, as in all the major cities of Brazil, there is a big difference between the lives of the rich and poor people.

Recife is a port, and many people work in offices that are connected with imports and exports. The airport employs hundreds of people in many different jobs. Recife's banks open for just a few hours every day. When they are open, they are very busy. All through the day you can see business people hurrying to and fro. Most of the shops open at 8:00 A.M. and do not close until 7:00 P.M. The bigger shopping centers stay open until 10:00 P.M. so that people with money can buy what they need in the evenings when it is cooler.

▽ **A Brazilian paints his jangada, or fishing boat, in Recife.**

Most jobs for people in the poor districts of Recife are temporary. There is never enough work to go around. People have to find any work they can. It is hard to earn enough money to live on. The poorer districts are often the farthest away from work. People who do have jobs have to leave their houses as early as 5:00 A.M. or 6:00 A.M. to take two or three buses to the city center.

Brazil has a small fishing industry, and most of it is in the north near Recife. Every morning Edison Nantes arrives at his local market with the fish he has caught that morning. Edison owns a traditional Brazilian fishing boat called a jangada. All jangadas used to be made from logs lashed together. Edison's is made from plastic tubes, which do not need painting.

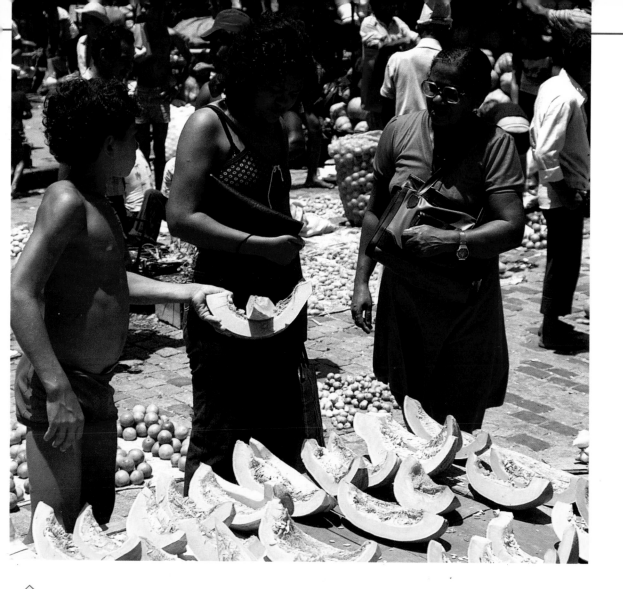

△ This boy is selling slices of melon from his stand in Recife's marketplace.

There are stands and markets all over Recife. There are many craftspeople who make pots, tableware, jewelry, and ornaments. The local market stands have things for people with money to buy. They are always well stocked with fresh produce, despite the drought.

Claudia, Edison's wife, is typical of many of the poorer women in Recife, who work as maids, clean house, or cook in the homes of wealthier families. Claudia spends her day washing, cleaning, and cooking for a family that works in one of the offices in the city. The richer people of Recife do not buy washing machines or dishwashers. It is cheaper to employ servants like Claudia. The very rich often have several servants—housemaids, a chauffeur, and sometimes a gardener. Those who live in big houses often employ armed guards to patrol their area.

School

In the poorer parts of Recife, many people work part time or have no job at all. Children have to try to earn some money, often by begging. Many do not go to school.

Many children in Recife shine shoes, clean windshields, or sell food in the streets. In the country outside Recife, they work on farms or in the home.

Over half of the children in Brazil go to private schools. Their parents are the people who have jobs in offices, banks, or factories in the cities, or who are landowners and farmers. There are many private schools in Recife. There are also "self-help" schools. These have been started by poor people to make sure that their children have some education. These schools do not have many books or other supplies. In school, as in the rest of life in Brazil, there is a rich world and a poor world.

△ A primary school class in Recife's neighboring town, Olinda.

Many adults who went to poor schools, or left school at a very early age, cannot read or write, or they have only very basic skills. The government knows this is a major problem. In order to help, it has set up adult education classes in the evenings. However, most people cannot see the point of taking classes because they will not always lead to a job. There are simply not enough jobs for everyone.

In parts of Brazil, Amerindian groups have their own education or training systems. The Kayapo and Shavante Indians live in reservations often far from their original lands. Their total population is only about 3,000. The men of the village have a council meeting and debating session every evening. During this meeting, village decisions are made. The boys are allowed to sit in and learn from their elders. By teaching their children themselves, these people can keep their traditions alive. The younger generations will know how to follow the tribal way of life. If they go to government schools, they may be influenced by Western ideas and modern lifestyles.

△ Children at this school in northeast Brazil have to wear a uniform.

Spare Time

In Recife most people have spare time on weekends, which they spend at the beach. On Sundays, in particular, everyone seems to be on the beach or ocean-front. There are parties with dancing and singing. Adults and children dance in the street in the midday sun. Some of the dances are called the samba, the lambada, and the bossa nova. In the northeast, a special form of the samba, called frevo, has developed over the years. The frevo is danced by solo dancers holding a small umbrella or parasol in one hand. It is a very fast and exhausting dance that has many knee bends and kicks, rather like a Russian Cossack dance.

The most important spare time activity for the people of Brazil is preparing for the carnival. In Recife, groups called Blocos practice all year round to be ready for the next carnival. The Blocos have names like "We Suffer but We Can Dance!" One Bloco has thousands of members, and they all get involved in the celebrations.

▽ **The streets are crowded for days during carnival time in Recife.**

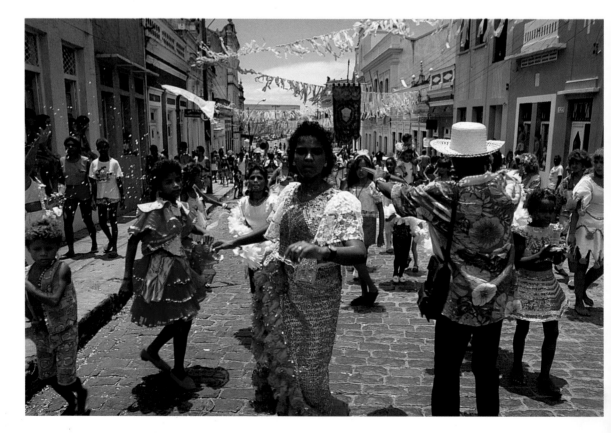

Originally the carnival was on Shrove Tuesday, the day before Lent. The idea was to use up all the energy, food, drink, and fun that would have to be forgotten during the somber period of Lent. Today it is a much longer event, lasting at least four days. It is also much noisier. The streets are packed with people in costumes, drinking, dancing, and singing. An essential part of any carnival celebration is drinking. The drinks are ice-cold beer and "cachaça," a strong drink made from sugar cane.

These carnivals in Recife are open to everyone. There is no entry fee.

Without doubt, soccer and volleyball are the most important parts of many young people's lives. Recife has three soccer teams. Brazil has won the World Cup three times. Also, the country has had perhaps the world's best player ever: Pelé. If Brazilians are not playing soccer, many will be watching. The Maracana stadium in Rio is the largest in the world. It is probably the noisiest and most colorful, too.

△ **The splendor of the Rio Carnival, the biggest carnival in Brazil.**

Katia's Day

Katia is eleven years old. She moved to Recife four years ago with her family, when the drought ruined the farm they worked on. Now she lives in a favela with her mother, Maria, and her four younger brothers and sisters. They are Paulo (nine), Claudia (seven), Patricia (four), and the baby, Pedro (one). Their father, also called Pedro, now lives with his brother in São Paulo. They are working in a new factory there. Sometimes Katia's father can send them some money, but it is never enough to live on.

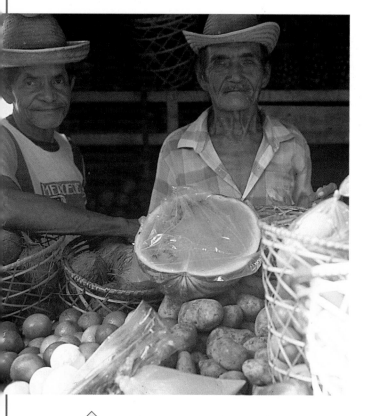

▲ Unlike Katia's mother, who has a cart, these men sell their fruit and vegetables from a stand.

Katia is always up by 6:00 A.M. Everybody gets up early in Brazil. Her first job is to make coffee for everyone. Next the younger children have to be cared for.

Because she is the oldest child, Katia helps her mother to prepare the sweet corn that they will take into the city to sell on the street. Katia's aunt collects Patricia and Pedro and takes them to her house. Katia takes the other children to school by 8:30 A.M. and then helps to wheel the cart to their usual spot on a street corner. She looks after the cart while her mother goes to collect laundry. The family washes other people's laundry to earn some more money.

At noon, Katia collects the children from school—their education is over for the day. She gives them their lunch of rice and beans before taking them to her aunt's house on the other side of the town. She then walks back to her mother's cart to take her some lunch, before walking 2.5 miles to school. She cannot afford to go by bus. The long walk means that she is often late for school, which begins at 1:00 P.M.

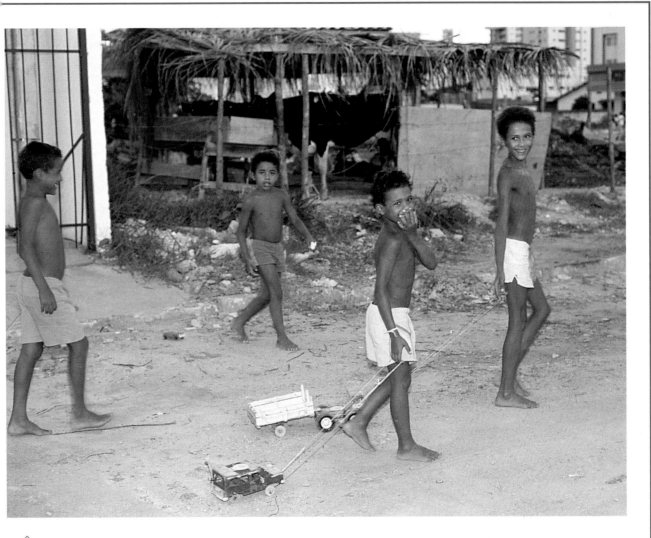

△ **These children are playing beside a favela in Recife.**

Katia's school "day" only lasts three hours. She studies Portuguese, history, geography, and math. Like a lot of her friends, Katia enjoys school. But she makes only poor progress because she cannot study at home and her family cannot afford to buy pens, paper, or books.

Just after 5:00 P.M. Katia arrives home after picking up the children from their aunt's. Katia keeps an eye on them as they play while she starts another job, washing the laundry her mother has collected earlier in the day. At around 8:00 P.M., after they have eaten, she takes all the children with her to meet their mother and helps to bring the cart home. Her mother finishes washing the laundry so that Katia can wash and bathe the children by pouring cold water over them from tin cans. Finally, Katia goes to bed, at about 9:00 P.M.

Traveling Around

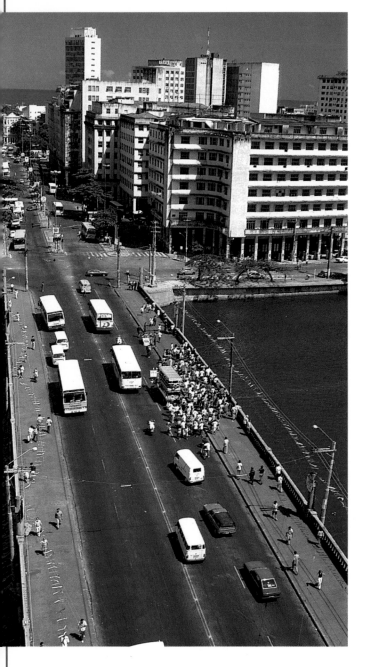

◁ Traffic crossing the Boa Vista bridge in Recife.

In the city center of Recife, there is always traffic and crowds of people. The pavements are packed with people setting up their stands and carts. They sell everything, from kitchen equipment to music. People with things to sell call out to passers-by.

There is always a lot of music. Shops and stands blare out music all the time. The "sound wagons" add to the street noise. These are loudspeakers on wheels, some as big as trucks. They are used to advertise goods, church services, or local politicians.

The streets are full of people selling. Children carry trays or handfuls of goods. They run after passers-by, clamoring for a sale. There are piles of fruit from the nearby country. The sellers spray water on the fruit to keep it looking attractive and to drive off the flies.

To get into or away from the city center, people crowd onto Recife's very good bus service. They can get to almost anywhere in Brazil by bus from Recife, as well as just around the city. Everyone has to go through a turnstile at the back of the bus when they pay to get on. Small children often crawl under the turnstile and travel free. On all the major streets, there are taxis that take people through the maze of winding streets in the city center.

The buildings in the center of Recife are a mixture of the old, grand Portuguese style and new blocks built in the 1970s. Many of the old-style buildings are crumbling. At night many people sleep near the cathedral or in doorways. In the daytime these people beg, or, if they are lucky, do odd jobs. Farther out, in the newer suburbs, people usually live in apartments. Because the climate is so warm, children can play outside all year round.

▽ **Some streets in Recife still have old, Portuguese-style buildings.**

In Recife, favelas are squeezed in almost anywhere, often between other buildings. The paths between the houses are narrow and twisting. There is no need for wide roads because no one there owns a car. In some places, there are planks to walk on because the ground is always wet.

Journeys

Brazil has a modern road transportation system. Since the 1960s, the government has borrowed a lot of money to build new roads, many through the Amazon Basin. The first one connected Brasília with Belém in the north. Another carries wood from the logging industry in the forest to the southeast. The latest is the Trans-Amazonian Highway. When it is finished, it will go from Recife in the east to the Peruvian border in the west. This highway will be 3,100 miles long.

In southern Brazil, there is a good local road network. However, in the north and in the Amazon Basin people can travel locally only by walking or by plane or boat. Many of the roads are not well built, so when the torrential rains come, they are washed away.

Buses are the least expensive way of traveling long distances. The regional bus services are excellent, and they go from city to city. The distances between cities are very long. To travel by bus from Recife to Belém around the coast in the northern states will cost about 27 dollars, and will take two days.

Traveling time can be shortened to a few hours by airplane. That is why there are hundreds of small airports all over Brazil. There are even airports deep in the Amazon Basin. All the major cities have big international airports. Travel by plane is the most expensive way to travel.

These Kaxinawa Indians are making their journey by boat.

Trucks and cars often have to rely on rafts like this one to cross Brazil's rivers.

In the Amazon Basin, river transportation is still important. For many river communities, the only link with the nearest town is by river. Because the Amazon River is so large, ocean-going ships can travel right up to Manaus in the center of the forest. There are specially built double-decker boats for long trips. These have enough room for people to hang their hammocks. Many people use canoes for short trips to pick up their provisions.

Not many Brazilians own cars, but those who do have a choice of different types of fuel. Some use gasoline and some use diesel fuel, but many run their cars on the alcohol fuel produced from sugar cane.

Looking at Brazil

Brazil today is a wonderful and complex mixture of the old and the new. There are modern cities with skyscrapers and airports. In the Amazon forest, Amerindian tribes follow traditions and a way of life that has not changed for thousands of years. There are rich landowners and huge multinational businesses. There are also thousands of poor people living in slums. Throughout the country's history, people have come to Brazil from all over the world, and this has made a rich, colorful mixture of customs and beliefs.

We always have images of a country in our minds, even if we have never actually been there. This book has tried to show many sides of Brazil. It has included some positive ideas and pictures about the country. It has shown what Brazilian people are doing to make a better life for themselves and their families.

◁ The carnival in Olinda.

▽ Brazilian soccer players in action.

△ Sunrise over Rio.

▷ Amerindian mother and child.

Brazil is a country rich in natural resources. It has enormous reserves of many important minerals, huge forests, and vast rivers. In the last fifty years, as part of an attempt to modernize the country, the government has decided to build a new capital city in Brasília and invest in new industries and roads to exploit this natural wealth. Unfortunately, this has led Brazil to build up huge debts to other countries and to cut down much of its rain forest. It has also meant that the wealthy landowners have grown richer, and there has been little benefit to the poor people. Oxfam and other development agencies have offered aid and helped people to organize themselves. Hard-working and determined Brazilians are trying to better their own conditions. By reading this book, you will have gained an insight into the lives of Brazilian people today.

Glossary

Amerindians The word is a combination of two words, "American" and "Indian," the original inhabitants of Brazil.

Colonists Groups of settlers or planters who left their own homes to live in new lands under the rule of their old countries.

Colonization When new settlers take over a country, or part of it, and claim it as their own, or for their own country.

Deforestation Clearing of all the trees and undergrowth in a forest to make land useable for farming.

Demarcation Putting down a boundary or a line marking out different areas of land.

Equatorial On or near the equator—the imaginary line that runs around the center of the earth.

Exporter A company or individual that buys or makes goods to sell abroad and not in the country where they are made.

Far East An area of the world made up of China, Japan, and other countries of East Asia.

Favelas Shanty towns in Brazil. The word comes from the Portugese word for slums.

Hardwood The wood from a deciduous tree (a tree which sheds its leaves every year—such as an oak) as opposed to wood from conifers (trees with needles).

Hydroelectric Electricity generated by using water power from dams.

Mahogany A dark, very hard wood, used for making furniture.

Nutrients Anything that contains the food or minerals needed to support living things.

Plantations An area of land, often called an estate, that was cultivated, usually with one crop like cotton or sugar cane.

Rain forest The dense forest that grows where there is always heavy rainfall, especially in the hot, tropical regions of the world.

Raw materials The basic materials, like wood and iron ore, from which finished goods are made.

Index

About Oxfam in Brazil

Oxfam America works in partnership with communities in Asia, Africa, the Americas, and the Caribbean to find long term solutions to poverty and hunger. Oxfam America supports the self-help efforts of poor people—especially women, landless farm workers, and survivors of war and natural disasters—who are working to make their lives better. Oxfam America believes that all people have the basic rights to earn a living and to have food, shelter, health care, and education.

Oxfam America is part of the international family of Oxfam organizations that work in more than 70 countries, including Brazil, where Oxfam's established program concentrates on the northeast and the Amazon basin—the country's poorest regions. Oxfam supports landless people, both rural and urban, by providing training, legal advice, and agricultural technology. Oxfam also helps people to claim their basic rights through work with community and women's groups and with trade unions, aiming to strengthen these organizations through leadership training. Oxfam is also helping poor people in Brazil to improve their living conditions by working with local groups to train health educators and literacy workers.

© 1996 Rigby Education
Published by Rigby Interactive Library,
an imprint of Rigby Education,
division of Reed Elsevier, Inc.
500 Coventry Lane
Crystal Lake, IL 60014

Printed in Hong Kong
Designed and produced by Visual Image
Cover design by Threefold Design

00 99 98 97 96
10 9 8 7 6 5 4 3 2 1

Library of Congress Cataloging-in-Publication Data

Marshall, David, 1945-
    Brazil / David Marshall.
        p.   cm. -- (Worldfocus)
    Includes index.
    Summary: Introduces Brazil's history, geography, culture, and economy, focusing on the city of Recife as an example of life in this Latin American country.
    ISBN 1-57572-029-9 (library)
    1. Brazil--Juvenile literature. [1. Brazil. 2. Recife (Brazil) I. Title. II. Series.
F2508.5.M276   1996
981--dc20   95-25034

Acknowledgments
The author and publishers would like to thank the following for their help with this book: The staff in the Recife office of Oxfam; Oxfam (UK and Ireland): Emma Naylor of the Brazil Desk and the staff of the Latin America and Caribbean Desk; the staff of the photo library; and the Oxfam Education staff who commented on early drafts.

The author and publishers also wish to acknowledge, with thanks, the following photographic sources:

Oxfam/Andrew Coulridge pp. 2, 4, 9, 15, 27; /Jenny Matthews pp. 3, 5, 6, 7, 12, 14, 18, 22, 23, 26; /F. Rubin pp. 8, 9, 29; /Tony Gloss pp. 11, 13; Reportage/Julio Etchart p. 10; South American Pictures/Tony Morrison pp. 16, 17, 20, 21, 24, 28; Hutchison Library p. 19; Andes Press Agency/Carlos Reyes p. 25; Allsport p. 28.

Every effort has been made to contact copyright holders of material published in this book. Any ommissions will be rectified in subsequent printings if notice is given to the publisher.

Cover photograph: © Oxfam/Mike Goldwater— Amerindian child